Embracing the Flame

Stories, Guidance, and the Path to Mastery

Bill Berry

All attempts have been made to preserve the stories of the events, locales, and conversations contained in this collection as the author remembers them. The author reserves the right to have changed the names of individuals and places if necessary and may have changed some identifying characteristics and details such as physical properties, occupations and places of residence in order to maintain their anonymity.

Published by Mr. Bill Berry

St. Petersburg, FL

www.mrbillberry.com

Design and composition by Bill Berry

Edited by Amy Kochek and Stephanie Gibson

Proofreading by Thom Wall, Carrie Matteoli, Mika Davis, and Nathan Wakefield

Photography by Steven Le, Thee Photo Ninja

Cover design by Robin Gunney

Print ISBN: 9798282743067

First Edition

Contents

Acknowledgments

♨ A YOGIC CIRCLE OF GRATITUDE ♨

Yama – External Integrity
• Ahimsa (Compassion / Non-Harming):
Steve – For showing me how easily fire can harm, and why exploration must be fierce, but never reckless.
• Satya (Truthfulness):
Amy – For slicing away ego and excess to reveal the truth in the work. The voice of clarity.
• Asteya (Non-Stealing):
Jonathan – We shared the dream and the spotlight, created original material, set impossible goals, and accomplished them all. We did it.
• Brahmacharya (Moderation / Right Use of Energy):
Joe Mystic – He lit the first wick.
• Aparigraha (Non-Attachment):
Marissa – A student now masterful in the flame. She took the teaching and made it her own.

Niyama – Internal Discipline
• Shaucha (Purity):
Catherine – Clear in form and thought, clean and sharp. She is

both flame and mirror, burning and reflecting, a voice for truth. (Special thanks for being our demonstrator in the "Techniques" chapter. And an extra special thank you to Amanda for photographing that session.)

- **Santosha (Contentment):**

Sue – My mother. Who never asked me to be anything else. In her eyes, I was always enough.

- **Tapas (Discipline / Fire):**

Noah – The fearless one, crafter of destiny, like a rocket on the pad just waiting to launch.

- **Svadhyaya (Self-Study):**

Mika – The teacher of words. Who made me examine not just what I say, but why.

- **Ishvarapranidhana (Surrender to the Divine):**

Stephanie – My partner. My forever flame. The divine I bow to in human form.

The Remaining Limbs: The Practice Embodied

- **Asana (Posture / Stability):**

Roger – My first fire juggling partner. We stood tall in a storm of sparks.

- **Pranayama (Breath Control):**

Jim – Who sent me on the first fire gig—the reason I even learned to breathe fire.

- **Pratyahara (Sense Withdrawal):**

Mimi – New seeker on the path. The first step is always inward. She took it bravely.

- **Dharana (Concentration):**

Robert & Johanna – The makers, able hands that forge our tools.

- **Dhyana (Meditation):**

Bill – My father - The union of the dream and creation. The meditation of craft into commerce. A dreamer who believed "it" could be done.

- **Anuvyavasāya (Layered / Perception):**
Carrie – The one who sees twice.
- **Samadhi (Bliss / Union):**
Me, Us, All – The work, the play, the fire, the breath. All of it—one.

"To the Ahimsa and the Satya, to the Tapas and the Dharana, to those who lit the torch and passed it—this is for you."

Bill - Matthew - Andrew - Mark - Byron - Carol - Bill - Tony - Keith - Matt - Dan - Jamie - Ivan - Bryson - Roni - Annette - Nathan - Joyce - Charlotte - Katie - Calvin - Tim - Sonya - Kelly - Erin - Adam - Fudge - Todd - Sean - Jeff - Thom - Jay - Meghan - Tina - Jessica - Bella Prana Collective - Kodawari - Ganesha Hot Yoga - Yoga 6 - Body Electric Yoga

"And to you, dear reader. For your belief, support, and bravery. May this process of discovery lead you to trust yourself more."
~Mr. Bill Berry

Chapter 1

DISCLAIMER

By purchasing, reading, using, or otherwise engaging with *Embracing the Flame,* you acknowledge and agree to the following terms and conditions:

1. **IMMERSIVE TRAINING EXPERIENCE**: *Embracing the Flame* is intended to serve as a supplementary resource to an in-person workshop or video training provided by Mr. Bill Berry or an instructor approved by him. It is not intended to be a standalone guide for learning the art of fire eating or fire manipulation.

2. **NO UNSUPERVISED FIRE MANIPULATION**: You agree not to attempt to manipulate or eat fire without first receiving direct, hands-on instruction from Mr. Bill Berry or an instructor expressly approved by him. Fire manipulation and eating are inherently dangerous activities and should only be attempted under controlled conditions with proper training.

3. **ASSUMPTION OF RISK**: You understand and acknowledge that fire manipulation and related activities (including but not limited to fire eating, fire breathing, and any other fire-related acts) carry significant risks, including the potential for serious injury, death, and property damage. You fully assume all risks associated

with engaging in such activities, whether or not explicitly mentioned in this agreement.

4. **RELEASE OF LIABILITY**: By engaging with *Embracing the Flame*, you hereby release, indemnify, and hold harmless Bill Berry, his instructors, agents, employees, affiliates, publishers, and any other individuals or entities associated with the creation, publication, or distribution of *Embracing the Flame* ("Released Parties") from any and all claims, liabilities, damages, injuries, losses, costs, and expenses (including legal fees) arising out of or in connection with your use of *Embracing the Flame* or participation in any related activities, including but not limited to fire manipulation or eating.

5. **COVENANT NOT TO SUE**: You covenant and agree not to initiate or participate in any lawsuit, claim, or action against the Released Parties related to the use of *Embracing the Flame*, fire manipulation or eating, or any injury, damage, death, or loss that may arise from your actions while engaging in fire-related activities.

6. **ENTIRE AGREEMENT**: This agreement constitutes the entire understanding between you and the Released Parties regarding the subject matter of this release and supersedes all prior communications or agreements, whether written or oral, relating to this matter.

7. **GOVERNING LAW**: This agreement shall be governed by and construed in accordance with the laws of the jurisdiction in which Mr. Bill Berry resides, without regard to its conflict of law principles.

By purchasing, reading, or using *Embracing the Flame*, you acknowledge that you have read, understand, and agree to the terms set forth in this disclaimer and release of liability.

Chapter 2

Meet Your Instructor

Hello! I'm **Mr. Bill Berry**, and I'm excited to guide you as you enter the thrilling world of fire manipulation.

I had my first experience juggling fire in 1997 when a street performer on the beach in Carlsbad, CA, unexpectedly pulled me into his show. Learning I was a juggler, he handed me flaming torches before a crowd and shouted, "Let's pass!" The audience roared in appreciation, and I walked away with heart racing and my first fire performance under my belt.

The combination of terror and excitement planted something deep in my soul, something that would eventually lead me to become a full-time entertainer, traveling the world, doing something I love.

As I write this today, my resume reads 85 countries, every US

5

state, thousands of shows, corporate events, colleges, and cruise ships; it's been a grand time filled with unbelievable experiences.

But now, I want to pass this knowledge on to the next generation of Trailblazers. Those who will take what's already been done and build on it anew. Yes, performers, yes, dreamers, but also yogis, truth seekers, boundary breakers, and those who wish to overcome their fears. There are countless lessons to be learned in the embrace of the flame. In these pages, I'll invite you to let the old burn away, making way for a bolder, braver you to emerge.

My Experience

Alongside my performing career, I'm also a **certified yoga teacher** with a particular interest in Pratyahara (the fifth limb) and the exploration of the mind-body connection. I like to blend the mindfulness and control of yoga with the dynamic, physical aspects of fire-eating and other explorative arts. This holistic approach makes my instruction stand out: you're not just learning tricks; you're mastering the mental discipline and physical control that make those tricks safe and effective.

Why I'm the Right Choice for You

This is where my years of professional performance experience, training in sword swallowing, and yoga practice come in. I don't just teach you how to manipulate fire; I teach you how to control your body, stay present, and overcome the natural fear of performing such an art.

My approach is about **empowerment**—providing the tools to safely explore your limits and bring your abilities to new heights. Whether it's one-on-one lessons or group sessions, I'll guide you with expertise, patience, and a true passion for these disciplines.

Let's ignite your journey; I'll be right here to lead you to your first breakthrough.

Mr. Bill Berry

Chapter 3

3 Months Free

Thank you for purchasing *Embracing The Flame*, the companion manual for Mr. Bill Berry's fire-manipulation workshop!

In these pages, you'll find valuable insights into the history of fire manipulation, along with essential guidance to help you develop this extraordinary skill safely and effectively.

To support your journey beyond the written word, the first 999 purchasers of this book receive a **free 3-month subscription** ($150 value) to the Mr. Bill Berry Patreon. This is not a sales pitch — it's a continuation of your training. Patreon is where you'll find video demonstrations, expanded techniques, and deeper explorations of the practices described in this manual.

I encourage you to take advantage of these resources and watch the techniques in action. This content is designed to help you go further, safer, and more confidently as you embrace the flame.

Redeem your **3 months** of access to the Mr. Bill Berry Patreon community today!

https://www.patreon.com/Mr.BillBerry/redeem/9E03C

Bill Berry

Chapter 4

A Rich History

Fire manipulation has been practiced for centuries, with its origins deeply embedded in various cultures worldwide. Historically, it was often part of ritualistic and spiritual traditions, symbolizing purification, mastery over the elements, and the transcendence of physical limitations. Over time, it transitioned from sacred ritual to spectacle, becoming a staple in street performances, circuses, and sideshows.

Key Historical Highlights:

Fire manipulation has intriguing connections to ascetic traditions, particularly among sadhus, jadoo-wallah, and fakirs. These practitioners were known for their extreme physical feats, demonstrating their spiritual discipline and ability to overcome the body's natural fear and pain responses. Here's a look at the key historical points that tie fire manipulation to these spiritual traditions:

1. Fire Manipulation and Ascetic Practices

Ascetics in India were known for performing extraordinary physical feats, including fire-related acts. These acts were believed to demonstrate their spiritual advancement and control over their physical senses. While fire walking and fire rituals were more common, some practitioners may have performed fire eating to demonstrate mastery over fear and pain.

Fire as a Symbol of Spiritual Power: Fire has long been a symbol of transformation and purification in Hindu and other spiritual traditions. Sadhus, who renounced worldly life to pursue spiritual enlightenment, often engaged in extreme austerities (tapas) to discipline their bodies and minds.

2. Tapas: The Role of Fire in Austerity Practices

Tapas, a Sanskrit term meaning "heat" or "austerity," refers to the self-discipline and spiritual effort undertaken by ascetics to purify themselves and attain enlightenment. Fire has been central to many ascetic practices, symbolizing both destruction and renewal.

Fire as Purification: Hindu ascetics have traditionally used fire in rituals such as homa (fire offerings) and acts of endurance, such as firewalking, as a means of self-purification. While direct references to fire eating are scarce, the principle of confronting and overcoming extreme physical challenges aligns with the broader tradition of tapas.

Testing Physical and Mental Limits: By engaging with fire, ascetics demonstrated their ability to transcend the physical body's limitations, a theme echoed in many yogic and spiritual disciplines.

3. Fire in Yogic and Shaiva Traditions

While fire eating is not explicitly mentioned in classical yogic texts, fire holds a significant place in Shaivism and broader Hindu traditions.

Shaiva Sadhus and Fire Worship: Devotees of Shiva, particularly Aghori sadhus, often engage in extreme rituals to break attachments to the physical world. Fire, as a representation of Shiva's destructive and transformative power, plays a central role in their practices.

4. Symbolic Connection to Pratyahara

Pratyahara, one of the eight limbs of yoga described in Patanjali's Yoga Sutras, involves withdrawing the senses to focus inward. While there is no historical evidence linking Pratyahara to fire eating, both practices emphasize control over sensory perception and the body's instinctive reactions. Fire eating has long been a display of physical and mental discipline, yet its deeper potential as a vehicle for internal transformation invites exploration.

For me, this exploration began long before I'd ever heard about things like fire-eating. As a child, I had a life-threatening heart condition, and my cardiologist, Dr. Raja Singham, introduced me to yogic principles as a means to regulate my heart—a lesson in mind and body control that would shape the rest of my life. He gave me tools that allowed me to redefine my limits entirely. He taught me how breath (Pranayama) and meditation (Dharana & Dhyana) could slow my pulse, how awareness could override the autonomic nervous system, and that the mind held far more influence over the body than most of us ever imagine. At an age when most kids were simply told to sit still, I was learning how to be still—internally, physically, and physiologically.

Those lessons in control found a home in my life's work, though at first, I didn't fully recognize it.

Sword swallowing, for example, requires an almost paradoxical mastery—one must be completely in control while simultaneously surrendering to the process. Through daily practice, I trained my body not to gag, my muscles not to resist, my breath not to falter. The same principles I had learned years before to slow my heart with breath and focus were now adapted to guide a blade past my throat's defenses. The same discipline that allowed me to override the body's automatic functions to control my heart, now allowed me to repress the gag reflex, and pass a sword into my body.

But it wasn't until I was on the yoga mat, years later, while attempting a particularly difficult posture, that these pieces fused into a singular realization.

Fire eating, sword swallowing, breath control, yoga, and even the ability to regulate my heart were not separate skills. They were different expressions of the same philosophy: the ability to master the body by mastering the mind. Pratyahara was not just a yogic concept; it was the thread that connected my entire journey. In that moment, I saw my work clearly—not as a collection of odd talents, but as a continuation of an ancient tradition, one where control, perception, and fear could all be transformed through deep, intentional practice.

This realization created a launchpad for new exploration. Fire eating, often seen purely as a performance, has the potential to be something more—a practice of deep internal control, a living embodiment of Pratyahara's essence.

My work resides in that space, revealing new dimensions of what the human body and mind can achieve. The flame is merely a gate; we must pass through it to discover what is on the other side.

Conclusion

The historical connections between fire and Indian ascetic practices highlight fire's long-standing role as a symbol of both spiritual and physical transformation. While fire eating is not explicitly documented as a yogic or ascetic practice, its underlying themes of endurance, purification, and transcendence align with the broader traditions of tapas and self-discipline. Perhaps one day, practices like fire-eating and sword-swallowing will find their way onto the mats and into the practice of modern yogis and meditators.

Chapter 5

Playing with Fire

Before we begin building your foundation, I want to take a moment to share how we've arrived here. My path with fire has been filled with hard-won lessons, close calls, and moments of deep insight. Fire has humbled me, empowered me, and taught me in ways no other element could. I've made mistakes, so you don't have to—and I've discovered techniques and rituals that I now pass on to my students. These stories aren't here to impress you; they're here to prepare you. Understanding where I've been will help illuminate where you're headed.

Fire is alive.

It breathes, hungers, and will do whatever it takes to survive.

Handling fire is like being a lion tamer in the ring. You must never turn your back on the big cat, never forget its power, and never fool yourself into thinking you're fully in control.

The following is a story about my first experience with fire. I hope that by reading it, you'll gain a deeper perspective on why I hold such deep respect for fire, stressing that you take your time while learning to work with it, to master it ultimately.

During the summer between my fifth and sixth grade school years, I hung out with my friend Steve almost daily. Our favorite thing was playing war in the trees and bushes around his house. So, when Steve's parents decided they wanted to install a below-ground swimming pool, they made us an offer. If we agreed to dig out a big hole where the pool would eventually go, his parents would wait until the following summer to move forward with the installation. In the meantime, they said we could use the hole to build an underground bunker to play war in. We, of course, jumped at the chance. Steve and his brother did a lot of the work, but a bunch of us neighborhood kids helped out, too. And in just a few weeks, a hole was dug out.

Next, we scrounged old materials from a nearby field to cover the hole. Then, we laid tarps down over the wood and spread a thin layer of dirt to camouflage everything. The "bunker" was complete. It was 5' deep, 10' wide, 15' long, and kidney-shaped, with one entrance and two different levels for the eventual shallow and deep ends.

It was lots of fun to play in, but it wasn't enough for Steve. He wanted to make the game more real. So, one day, he started experimenting with any combustible materials or flammable chemicals that he could find. I asked him about it, and he said he wanted to make napalm. Each time he completed a new chemical concoction, the fort became an impromptu laboratory for conducting "tests." It seemed harmless, and Steve claimed to know what he was doing, but I always stayed outside while he was burning stuff. I didn't even feel comfortable striking matches, so I sure wasn't going down in the hole where the fire was.

After a few weeks, Steve decided to improve his concoctions by adding gasoline to the mix. I was visiting when he tested this out for the first time. As usual, I sat right outside the entrance to watch. He began by lighting a small brush fire on the fort's floor. Then he picked up a large plastic bottle filled with gasoline and slowly poured it onto the flames. The fuel was so combustible that the flames raced up the stream into the full bottle and then exploded.

The entire interior of the fort was instantly engulfed in flames!

I leaped backward in fear, the heat searing even though I was several yards away. In a panic, I ran away from the fort. Behind me, I could hear him screaming, but I was too blinded by terror to stop. I got to my bicycle and was about to jump on when my brain kicked back on. My instant thought was, "What if he burns to death?" I hesitated for a second, not knowing what to do.

I heard him scream again, "Billy, help!"

I turned around and sprinted back towards the fort. When I got there, flames were billowing out of the entrance, and I couldn't see Steve at all. I dropped to my knees and started throwing dirt through the opening as fast as possible. The fire died down a little, and I could see Steve huddled in the deep end behind a wall of flames. He was completely frozen with shock, with fire glinting in his glazed-over eyes. It was surreal, like a scene in a horror movie. I kept throwing dirt until a gap appeared in the flames. As soon as Steve saw this opportunity, he recovered enough to make a break for it, nearly bowling me over in his rush to escape.

Now that he was safely outside, we joined forces, throwing dirt wildly until the fire was completely out.

With a feeling of relief, we stood up and shakily looked at each other.

Looking down, he said, "My leg," and started to limp toward the house. I walked beside him, unsure how to help.

A few steps later, he began to whimper, then he quickened his steps.

Whimpers turned to shouts, and he began to run.

Before we made it to the back door of his house, the numbing effects of adrenaline had worn off, and he broke into a full sprint, screaming maniacally as he went.

I tried to follow him inside, but he locked me out.

I went around to the front of the house, but the front door was locked, too.

I knocked and knocked, but he didn't answer. I could hear him screaming inside, and I didn't know what to do, so I kept knocking.

Finally, he opened the door. His face was transformed by pain, cheeks streaked by tears. Between screams, he shouted, "Go home!" Then he slammed the door in my face.

Still not knowing what to do or how I could help, I finally walked over to my bicycle and rode home. When I arrived, my mom saw my colorless face and knew something was wrong, but I didn't tell her what happened and went to my room.

A few hours later, Steve's parents called and told my mom what had happened.

Steve had been rushed to the emergency room. The doctors diagnosed second and third-degree burns on large swaths of his legs. He would have to undergo multiple skin grafts over many months to repair the damage. And that while recovering, he'd have to keep his burns out of the sunlight for two years until the skin was fully regenerated.

The traumas of that day drove a friendship-ending wedge between Steve and I. One so complete, we never spoke again.

To this day, when I think of Steve, I see him in that doorway—his tear-streaked, pain-ridden face screaming at me, 'GO HOME!!!' Then the door slams.

That movie plays in my mind as vividly today as it did when it happened 40 years ago.

I learned what happens when fire is not given the respect it deserves.

Chapter 6

Clarence the Dragon

Knowing what **not** to do is as important as knowing what you should.

One day, while sitting in my 10th-grade science class, I noticed Clarence, a classmate, doing something strange. His fist was pressed up against one nostril, and it looked like he was concentrating really hard or hiding something. His eyes were locked on the girl in the row next to him, giving her this wild, twitchy look like he was inviting her into a secret.

She eventually noticed him and raised an eyebrow, clearly confused.

Then I noticed something colorful and oval shaped poking out the back of his hand. I recognized this shape as the base of a cigarette lighter, but knowing that brought me no closer to deciphering his intentions.

Is he sniffing the gases? I wondered silently.

A few seconds passed.

Clarence gave one last deep inhale and then, very matter-of-factly, struck the flint.

Fwoom!

His entire sinus cavity, which he'd been flooding with butane gas, ignited.

Twin jets of flame shot out of each of his nostrils like some kind of fire-breathing dragon. Clarence's face contorted in an expression of fiery regret. He flailed in his chair, shaking his head like a dog that had tried to eat a bee and immediately realized its mistake.

The girl screamed. The teacher spun around. And Clarence, with eyes watering and nostrils smoldering, tried to pretend he wasn't the poster child for science experiments gone wrong.

It remains one of the most recklessly stupid uses of fire I've ever had the misfortune to witness.

Chapter 7

Trial by Fire

No one is ever truly ready for their first experience working with fire. It's normal to be terrified the first time, to doubt yourself, and think, "I don't know if I want to do this."

Every student I've worked with has expressed those same concerns—until they step into it, trust the process, and feel the flame.

Once they do, they want more.

And I get it. I was drawn back to it once I'd experienced it for the first time.

The following story will tell how I found myself there, juggling fire for the first time.

I'd heard about a juggler who street performs on Carlsbad Beach and decided I needed to find him.

There's no real plan—just a vague hope that I'll spot him practicing in a park or catch sight of the VW Bus I've heard he lives in. So I make trip after trip, driving up and down the coast, weaving through side streets, scanning for some guy tossing clubs in the air.

Nothing.

I keep trying, but the weeks go by without any luck. There's no way to look him up or track him down. He's a ghost.

I give up.

Then, two weeks later, I'm at the beach with my girlfriend, watching the sunset, and there he is. Setting up for a show.

Finally.

We walk over, and I introduce myself as a juggler. He looks me over, sizing me up.

"Can you pass clubs?" he asks.

"A little," I say. "My friend and I have done it a few times."

"Can you juggle torches?"

"Oh no, I've never done that."

"But you juggle clubs, right?"

"I do."

"Alright, then you can juggle torches."

Without another word, he turns to the dozen people sitting on the concrete seawall and shouts, "This guy's a juggler! So we're gonna do something special—we're gonna juggle these!"

He lifts a set of well-used juggling torches into the air. "We're gonna light these on fire, then pass them between us."

The crowd leans in, intrigued. He launches into a bit about needing a lighter, borrowing one from the audience, slipping it into his pocket, and then asking for another. When someone else offers one, he takes it, and then with a grin, he pulls the first one back out, getting an easy laugh from the crowd.

He flicks the lighter, and the torches roar to life.

He tosses me one. I catch it. Two more, and it's go time.

He yells the universal signal for *we're starting*, "Hup!"

We start.

From the moment I make the first throw, I feel the difference. And I don't mean the heat; the flames create drag, shifting the weight of the torches. Every throw feels unpredictable.

I should be terrified of the fire. But I'm more afraid of messing up in front of all these people. The fire, intense as it is, pales in comparison to the pressure of the audience's eyes on me.

Then, as soon as I think I'm getting the hang of it, I drop one.

Doh.

I scramble to pick it up, and we keep going. The crowd cheers, impressed despite the mistake.

Roger yells, "Hup," again, so I stop.

And just like that, I've performed fire in front of an audience for the first time.

Roger takes over from there, launching into the rest of his show. He's got all kinds of cool tricks, but his big finale is the best—he balances on a giant green walking globe while juggling the torches.

I drop five bucks into his hat when he finally takes his bow. "Great show," I tell him. Then, hoping this might lead somewhere, I add, "Would you want to get together and practice sometime?"

He smiles appreciatively but shakes his head. "These days, the show itself is my practice."

Then a woman walks up, and he shifts gears instantly, flashing a grin and flirting with her. Within minutes, they plan to meet at a bar after he packs up.

I don't want to give up just yet, so I throw out one more offer. "Well, what if we did a show together sometime? I could help you juggle fire."

Roger pauses, then picks up his black top hat and holds it out so I can see inside.

There's maybe forty bucks in there—maybe less.

"There's not enough money in there for me," he says. "So there's definitely not enough for both of us."

I nod. I get it.

"Thanks anyway," I say, then turn and walk away.

Chapter 8

Meeting a Master

Working with fire changed my life, and doors that otherwise would have remained closed began to open. In this story, I'll tell you about one of these doors and give you a glimpse into the opportunities that arise when we step out of the familiar and embrace the flame.

Juggling fire with Roger the beach juggler showed me that I needed to keep expanding my skillsets to have any hope of performing professionally, including adding fire torches to the repertoire. So, I flipped through a juggling catalog a friend had given me that I knew offered fire props. I picked out the juggling torches I wanted, then noticed on the same page a product I'd never even heard of before: "Fireballs."

From my earliest juggling explorations, I'd always been partial to ball juggling, so the idea of juggling flaming balls was too good to pass up, and I impulsively added a set of three to my order sheet.

Then, I wrote out a check, sealed up my order and payment in an envelope, sent it off, and waited impatiently for everything to arrive.

When the box showed up, I immediately went out in front of my apartment to try out the Fireballs. They were essentially a spiral ball of wire dipped in silicone to dissipate some of the heat. Each ball had metal caps on each end where the wicks were attached to the hollow inside part of the ball. The caps had a small hole where you'd inject fuel to saturate the wicking tucked inside the caps. Then, when you light it, the fire licks out from the inside.

Lighting them up, I juggled them for the first time. The shape, size, and feel of the balls made any sort of advanced trickery challenging. And though the silicone wrapping helped, they didn't stay cool for long. Anything more than 30 seconds, and your hands began to burn.

Hmm, not the most practical props I decided, but still, I'm glad I understand how they work. I blew them out and started fueling them a second time. As I did, I heard a man's voice from the second-story window of the apartment next to the one I lived in. The voice said, "Is that hard to do?

I looked up but couldn't see anyone through the window screen; I asked, "Do you know how to juggle?"

He shouted back, "Yes."

"Well, if you can already juggle, it's essentially the same. You just have to keep them moving so you don't burn your hands. Do you want to try?"

"I do," he said, "I'll be right down."

I continued my refueling exercise and heard the sound of a door closing nearby. Then, a Hispanic-looking man with short-cropped dark hair approached. He wore a plain black T-shirt, loose-fitting black cotton pants, and slipper-like black shoes that looked like they might be made of felt. I guessed he was in his mid-30s, and he spoke with no accent.

"Do you want to try with some regular beanbags first to warm up?" I asked.

"No, I want to juggle those," he said, pointing at the Fireballs.

With anyone else, I might have insisted he try the balls first, if

34

only to see that he was, in fact, a competent juggler. But there was something in his manner, a confidence in his stride, so I didn't argue.

He reached out his hands for the Fireballs, which I gave him. Then I lit them, and he started juggling—quite competently, in fact.

"Have you juggled fire before?" I asked while he was still juggling.

"No, never!" he laughed.

"Well, that's pretty good." As I said this, he dropped, I'd broken his concentration by talking to him. But I quickly grabbed the drop and handed it back so he could continue.

"Man, they're starting to get hot!" He said.

"Yeah, stop anytime you want to, or just drop them, and we'll extinguish them."

"Ok, here, I'll throw you one," He said, throwing me one simultaneously.

I caught it and, with a big blast of breath, extinguished the flame.

He copied me and blew out the other two before handing them back.

"Thank you," he said, "that was exhilarating."

"Of course," I said. Then asked, "Did you just move in? I thought that apartment was empty?"

"No, we've been here for four years now."

"Really? We've been here for a while, too, but I've never seen you."

"Well, we keep to ourselves mostly. So why are you out here juggling? I see you almost every day with your unicycle and stuff?"

"I want to be a professional, perform, do gigs, maybe even compete in the world championships one day. At least, that's the dream." As I said this, I absentmindedly, and with a wince, reseated my right shoulder into its socket.

Noticing this, he asked, "What's wrong with your shoulder?"

"Oh, nothing. It's stupid, really. I tried to slam-dunk a basketball one time in high school, and it's been a little fussy ever since."

"Ah, well, since you let me juggle, let me do something for your shoulder, it'll help it heal. Come with me." Then he turned and began to walk towards his house. His tone was one of authority; he wasn't asking me, yet there was no threat in his tone, and I felt completely safe. So I followed him up the walkway and into his home.

There were no lights on inside, so the home was dim, illuminated only by the trickles of light that had wormed their way through the holes and creases of the window's horizontal blinds. There was a distinct herbal medicine smell, like a cross between Vicks Vapo Rub and an Asian restaurant, but not unpleasant, just crisp. Looking into the living room, I was surprised there was no furniture, not even a table; the floor was completely clear. But there were dozens of black and white, 8x10 photographs ringing the living room. I walked over and looked at the first photograph, and was surprised to see a very old Asian man standing next to Arnold Schwarzenegger. Then I went to the next photo and the same old Asian man was next to Jean-Claude Van Damme, the next was Chuck Norris, then Bruce Lee, Jackie Chan, Sylvester Stallone, and on and on. Every action hero you could think of was on the wall. My host said nothing as I did this; he just watched.

I've never been one to get star-struck; I can appreciate people's work without being a fool about it, but this was admittedly pretty incredible. Then my new friend spoke over my shoulder, "Do you notice that they are all standing behind him in every photo?"

I had not noticed before, but I did now that he was pointing it out. "Why is that?"

"It's a sign of respect," he answered. "In Chinese tradition, you stand behind whoever is the most respected and revered of the group."

"Why is he with all these people?"

"Because he is Shifu; he is their teacher."

"Teacher of what?" I asked.

"Many things."

"Is he your teacher?"

"He is."

"What did he teach you?"

My new friend looked at me, or maybe it was through me, like he could see something more than eyes alone are intended to see.

"I want to show you something," then he walked up the stairs to the second floor. I followed, somehow knowing it was what he'd intended.

He opened the door to one of the bedrooms, and I followed. As I passed the threshold, I was stunned by the simplicity, complexity, and how those contradictory descriptions seamlessly combined in this one space. To the right was a small, simple bed. No frame, no blanket, just a sheet over a narrow mattress. A small nightstand was beside the bed, with one or two personal items on top. Under the window was a low-slung table with a decorative cloth across its top. On this table were two black and white, 8x10 photos of my new friend. In both, he wore a black Gi and practiced martial arts. Next to this table on the floor was a simple cloth sack nestled inside a short wooden box. Then, my eyes began to scan the walls. Hanging on simple nails was every martial weapon imaginable. Swords, sai, a bo staff, nunchucks, a chain with a heavy metal handle attached, a three-sectional staff with chains linking the sections, various knives, and more. And none of these items looked like the cheap flea market. *Look how cool I am; I bought a sword,* type junk.

These were legitimate weapons.

"Do you know how to use all these?" I asked.

"Yes, weapons are my specialty. He.." he motioned down the hallway as he said this, "thinks I have too many, says it brings bad energy to have them, but I don't care, I like 'em." Then he picked up two pairs of nunchucks and began to move. These chuks had wooden handles connected by nylon cordage, so as he worked, the only sound they made was the sound of the air being cut; the speed he generated with his swings was dazzling. He swung them high and low, turning side to side and doing it all in a tiny space without hitting the walls or giving me the slightest sense of fear. He was in absolute control of the weapons.

"Man, I've never seen anyone move them that fast. My brother had a set years ago that he'd play with, but nothing like this."

Without slowing his movement, he asked, "Did your brother's set have cordage or chain linking the handles?"

"His were chain," I answered.

"Yeah, chain is clunky, loud, and slow. And you can wear through the metal; cordage is the way to go."

"You can wear through the metal?" I asked skeptically.

Still chucking at lightning speed, my friend looked at me and nodded, "Yes, I've worn through several sets of chains."

Given his matter-of-fact tone and obvious mastery, I didn't doubt it. Reaching into my pocket, I pulled out a pack of gum. "Want one?" I asked.

"Sure," he said, "You can put mine on the table."

I did so, then unwrapped mine and put it in my mouth. Then I looked around for a trash can for the little silver foil wrapper.

"Hey," he said, "ball that wrapper up and throw it at me."

"Ok," I said, wadding it up, "just say when."

"Whenever you like," he answered.

"Anytime at all?"

"Yep."

I held the wrapper in my hand, watching as the handles of his Chucks whizzed by at skull-crushing speeds. Then, when he seemed relatively committed to a complex sequence, I quickly threw the wrapper at him.

THWAAP, he batted the wrapper straight back at me.

"Pick it up," he ordered.

I did, then threw it again, this time harder.

THWAAP, he knocked it away again. I was stunned.

"Pick it up," he repeated.

This continued, and I threw it several more times, but each time he defended perfectly, effortlessly. I'd of called it some "Matrix-level shit," except this was 1997 and that movie wouldn't be released until 1999.

From down the hallway, I heard a voice yell angrily, "Hay, whut yu doin! No fighting!!"

"We're not fighting," my friend retorted, "I'm just showing him some stuff."

A little old Asian man, maybe in his 60s, but definitely the man from the photos downstairs, leaned his head in through the doorway to look at me. Then he told me, "Yu tell him tu, no reason all these weapon. Yu tink this help yu bad guy come?"

My friend answered, "Yeah, I'm about to drive off a bad guy right now." Then, he turned and assumed a fighting stance toward the old man.

The old man's eyes widened, then he shouted, "Oh, yu wanna mess wit me mudduh fukkuh?! Yu tink yu bad!" He turned and marched down the hall with purpose, then returned a moment later, waving a large semi-automatic pistol. "Yu tink yu toys stop a bullet, yu tink yu gang banger?!"

My friend dropped his nunchucks and held his hands up placatingly, but the old Chinese man continued to push him and yell at him threateningly. My friend fell to the ground with hands raised to defend himself, so the old man looked at me and said, "Yu see eveyting, it self defence, he attack me." Then he turned back to my friend and shouted, "I kil yu, I don't care, better than what happen I not find yu! Stupi Mexican!"

Now, they both broke out laughing, the kind that occurs between the closest of friends. Somehow, even though I didn't know either of these men who were brandishing deadly weapons, I never once felt any fear; there was mirth in the exchange.

The old man offered my friend his hand and helped him up, then he looked at me. "Whu yu?"

My friend answered for me, "He's our neighbor. He let me juggle, so I brought him up. His shoulder is hurt. Can you help him?"

"Ohhhh, I see yu on funny bicycle."

My friend jumped in again, "It's a unicycle."

"No, funny bicycle, I say, yu say **yes** Shifu."

"Yes, Shifu," my friend answered.

Looking back at me, he said, "Wish shoulder?"

I pointed to my right one, and he grabbed at my shirt, tugging it he said, "Take off."

Then, to my friend, he said, "Get Jow."

My friend responded, "There's some in the drawer."

Opening the drawer of the tiny table next to the bed, the old man saw many jars and began to shout again, "Five jar, yu steal from me!"

My friend again laughed and said, "No! Well, yes, but I need them!"

"Five jar! Yu tief, never change!"

I had my shirt off, and the old man grabbed my shoulder and moved it through its normal range of motion. He did not ask me what happened or where it hurt; he could feel everything he needed to. And to my surprise, his inspection was painless. Then he lifted my arm and had me hold it just so, then he lifted under my arm and, with a quick jerk, seated it more deeply than I'd been able to myself. "How feel?" he asked.

I moved my arm up and down a little, then said, "Wow, it's great, thank you."

"Good," he answered, then he unscrewed the cap from one of the jars and began to rub a strong medicine-smelling ointment into my shoulder. "This make heal," he said.

"What is it?" I asked.

"Dit Da Jow," he said in a tone that indicated everyone in the world knew what that was.

"Oh," I answered.

When he'd finished rubbing in the ointment, he told me, "No shirt, Jow stain."

I nodded and thanked him, and then he left.

Looking at my friend, I asked, "How'd he know how to fix my shoulder?"

"He apprenticed under a Chinese doctor when he was young."

"So he's a doctor and a martial artist—that's impressive," I said.

"And a farmer, a blacksmith, a politician, and a diplomat. His father sent him to live with other masters for training; it was the old way."

"He'd go live in other people's houses? Like a worker?"

"No, like a son. And the sons from these other families would go to live with his father to do the same. All families of the aristocracy did this; it created political stability and deep bonds. When those boys grew to be men and were charged with ruling the country, they would be less likely to go to war with a family that had once taken them in and treated them as one of their own. It was that way for centuries, but then Mao Zedong came to power and began his revolutionary purges. My Shifu was young then, so he fled; he escaped over the wall, and eventually made his way to England. After a few years there, he received a letter from the queen that granted him special passage to the US."

"The Queen gave him a letter?"

"Yes," he said, standing up and walking into the hallway. He lifted a framed picture off the wall where it had been hanging and held it out for me to see.

Under the glass was a very ornate and official-looking legal document; it had a picture of a woman wearing a large crown, whom I ventured to guess was the queen. All of the writing was hand calligraphic and looked a little like the copies I'd seen of the US Constitution, but much fancier. At the bottom of the document was a signature in ink, differently colored from the rest of the writing. I didn't have time to actually read it, but it looked exactly how I'd expect a Queen's letter to look.

"So he came to the US, then what?"

"He opened a school teaching martial arts, and when he was discovered, he started choreographing fight scenes for action movies. Right around then, he found me. I was just a street kid getting into trouble, fighting, and stealing, and I didn't have anybody. So he took me in, set me straight, and I've been with him ever since."

"Like he'd been taken in by those other families," I said.

"Yeah, just like that," he said.

"Okay, explain this to me, then. How did he climb the wall and escape if he was just a little kid? He's what, 60 years old, maybe 65?"

My new friend laughed at this, "65?! Try 85!"

"He's 85? No friggin way, he looks way younger."

My friend looked at me and asked, "How old do you think I am?"

"Mid 30's?"

He laughed again, "I'm 53."

"No way," I exclaimed, "how? You both look so much younger."

My friend cupped his hands together, and I could tell he was trying to think of how to explain something complex but in a quick and easy way.

"We eat simple, exercise, regular training, meditation, the things you'd expect. But it's also important to balance the body's Chi."

"What is Chi?"

"The body is made of energy, and with training, you can learn to control that energy."

"Right," I said; despite what I'd seen so far, I could not hide my skepticism.

Reaching under the table by the window, he slid out a couple of magazines that had been stowed there. The covers said "Kung Fu Magazine." Opening one of them, he quickly found a page and held it out to me to read. On it were a series of black and white photos showing his Shifu standing in a robe holding a coconut. Then, in the next photo, he raises his arm; in the next, his arm is traveling down with such speed that the camera only catches the blur; in the next, the coconut explodes from the impact, sending shards and liquid spraying out. Then, on the next page, there was another series of images, which were of the old man's hands. I couldn't figure out what was happening except that the latter photos looked foggy. "What's happening in these pictures?" I asked.

"He's focusing his Chi energy, generating so much heat that his fingertips are smoking."

I looked even more closely at the photos. The quality wasn't the best, kind of grainy, so I didn't really believe it was smoke. Plus, now that I was studying juggling and magic, I'd learned some of the techniques magicians used to do their tricks. So I just figured the old shifu was mixing in a bit of trickery for show. But that said, everything else I'd seen had been exactly what they'd said it was, impossible as the story seemed.

"Ok, seriously, how does one train that?"

"Well, one way is to learn Iron Palm. That's what he's doing with the coconut in the photo, but it takes a long time, lots of discipline, and a lot of Jow."

"So what is Iron Palm, and what is Jow made from? Is it like Tiger Balm?"

"Jow is an herbal ointment made from special or even secret ingredients. There is a similar version you can buy here in the US, and yes, there's Tiger Balm, but neither of those is the real stuff, so he makes his own, which is why he gets so mad when I take the jars."

"And Iron Palm?"

"See that bag over there?" He pointed to the cloth sack next to the table that I'd seen earlier. "Pull it out from the wall and kneel in front of it."

I did as he instructed.

"Now, hit it with the palm of your hand."

I did, "Ouch, that's hard!"

"Yes, it's currently filled with small river stones. But when you begin, it's filled with sand, and you strike it with the right palm, left palm, right butt of hand, left butt of hand, right back of hand, left back of hand, then roll your hand over, tuck away the thumb, and hit it with the knife edge of the top of each hand." He demonstrated as he explained. "Now you try; just do it softly at first."

Sitting straight, I began to repeat the pattern, hitting the bag with my right then my left, slowly gaining in speed and confidence as I fell into the pattern.

"Yes, just like that, now breathe," he said.

"How long do I have to do it?" I asked.

"A year," he answered.

"A YEAR!" I stopped hitting it.

"Yes, and each month, you change the filling, gradually making it harder and harder. So you start with sand, then small pebbles, wood chips, small river stones, etc., and by the end, you can do it with a solid piece of rock. But you have to rub Jow into your hands every day, breathe, meditate, and not miss any days because if you do, you have to start over."

"And you've done this all the way through?"

He nodded, "Several times."

"And then you can break coconuts with your bare hands?"

"I've seen a guy who could punch holes in cinder blocks after becoming a specialist in Iron Palm."

"And he didn't get hurt?"

"No, but he used real Jow. People here try to do it without having access to real Jow, and they mess themselves up."

I was deeply fascinated by all this, but I noticed that the light coming through the blinds had dimmed. I'd lost track of time, and the sun was going down while all of my juggling props were still out in the front area. "Hey, I don't mean to run, but it's getting late, and I gotta go grab my juggling stuff."

"Yeah, alright, but I have a question for you: why don't you believe in Chi energy?"

"I was raised Christian, I believe in that and nothing else," I said confidently.

"Do you know what Jesus' primary message to the world was?" he asked.

"None come unto the Father but through me?" I answered.

"Yes, he said that, but no, what was his real message?"

"Uh, I dunno," I answered.

"Be cool," he said.

"Be cool?" I asked.

"Yeah, be cool. Love your neighbor as yourself—that's being cool. Don't steal or covet—be cool. Treat others as you want to be treated—be cool. In fact, if you study any major religion that has ever existed, they all have the same message: Be cool."

"I've never thought of it that way," I said.

"Well, it's just something to think about." He stood up and headed for the stairs, so I got up to follow him.

As we reached the bottom and turned towards the exit, he said, "I really appreciate you letting me juggle the Fireballs, so I want to show you something. This is not something I ever show anyone, that's not what it's for, but I think you'll understand."

Stepping into the kitchen, which was now quite dark, he raised both of his hands in front of himself. Then, he began to breathe deeply, loudly, and with purpose. With each inhale, he would rub his fingertips together the way you might if you were balling up a paper straw wrapper. Then, on the exhalation, he would slowly separate fingers, drawing them outward the way one might if they were wrapped round with a heavy rubber band. He repeated/continued the exercise for about 30 seconds; then I began to see little flashes of light emanating from his fingers, like tiny LEDs that darted along the lines of his fingerprints. He intensified his breathing, and the light became brighter; now, when he separated his fingers on the exhalations, the fingerprint pads of all ten of his fingers actively glowed. Not like a flashlight, not like some manmade source would. It was delicate, the way a grouping of fireflies would light up if they all turned on at once, or how the bioluminescent algae look when they're illuminating the surf off San Diego during a full moon. It was magical. He continued the demonstration, and on the final handful of breaths, I saw tiny sparks fly between his fingers, similar to how you can occasionally see the spark from a shock of static electricity if you discharge it in dim enough light. Then, his breathing began to normalize, and as he did so, the light in his fingers dissipated. A few more moments passed, and he stood still in front of me, hands still raised in front of himself, and then he opened his eyes.

I spoke first, "I mean no disrespect, but would it be ok if I felt your hands?"

Without a word, he held his hands a few inches closer to me, indicating his blessing.

I reached up and felt his fingers, feeling the tips where the light had been, searching for some glow-in-the-dark fluid or some tiny device that could have emitted the light. But there was nothing there —nothing that could have created the effect, and his hands never left my sight. I dropped my hands in puzzlement.

"How?" I asked, dumbfounded.

He said nothing, only looked at me.

"It's real?" I asked, though it wasn't a question.

"Yes," he said simply.

"How?" I asked again.

"The mind and body are more powerful than you can imagine, but they must be trained."

I nodded, hoping I'd understood, but not certain that I had. Then, I turned and walked toward the front door. Stepping outside, I turned back to look at him once more, "Thank you; you've given me much to think about."

He nodded and started closing the door, but I stopped him. "Hey, what's your name anyway?"

He looked at me and said, "Miguel. What's your name?"

"Bill," I answered.

"Bill," he repeated, then he gently closed the door.

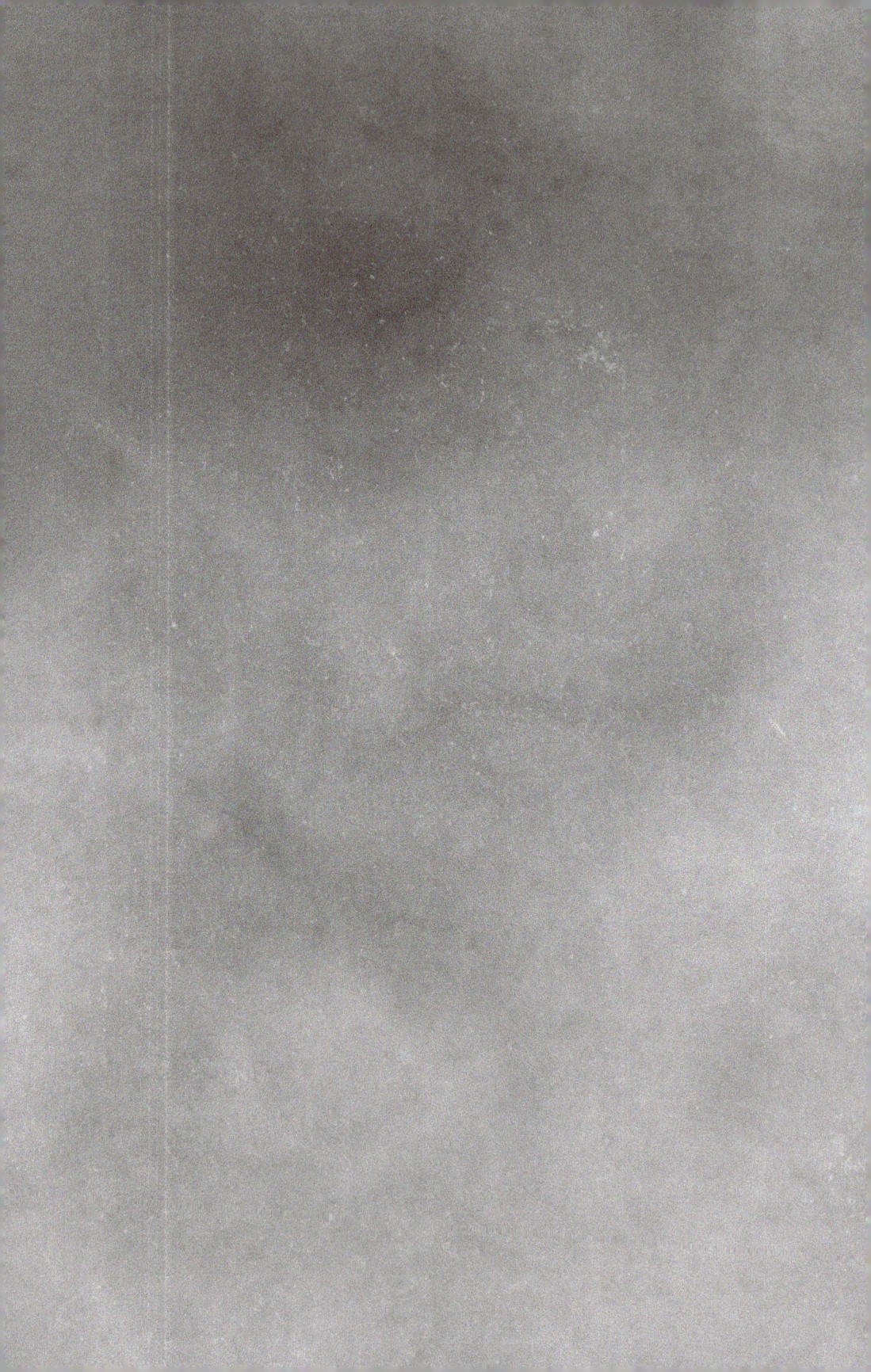

Chapter 9

Three Alarm Fire

In this story, I'll tell you about my first fire-eating gig.

Back then, there was no clear path for learning fire eating—you figured it out, pieced things together, and took your lumps along the way.

Luckily, today, the path is different. You can purchase quality equipment, train with a mentor, and connect with fire enthusiasts worldwide. You don't have to stumble in the dark like I did.

::*ring ring*::

Reaching for the corded phone, I pick it up. "Hello?"

"Hey Bill, it's Jim with Sparkles the Clown. We've got a request for a fire eater. Is that something you do?"

"Hey, Jim. Yeah, I can do that."

"You can do all the tricks? Eat it and everything?"

"Yep, not a problem."

"Okay, great. The gig is in two weeks and pays $200 for a 45-minute show. I'll get you the rest of the details once it's confirmed."

49

"Sounds good, thanks. Say hi to Lauren (Sparkles) for me."

"Will do. Talk soon. Bye."

"Bye."

I hang up and jot down the details on my massive three-foot-wide paper calendar. *Sweet. Two hundred bucks for 45 minutes of work.* Not long ago, I was making $5.50 an hour making pizzas, so $200 is serious money.

And I can't afford to turn it down just because I don't know how to eat fire... How hard could it be?

I've got two weeks to figure it out. All I have to do is find a mentor, buy the materials to make torches, learn the skill, and be ready to perform in 13 days.

I've only ever seen one person eat fire in real life—my friend Daniel—but I don't think he'd teach me.

But another local juggler I'd recently met, Jonathan, once mentioned a magician he worked with who ate fire, a guy named Joe Mystic.

Maybe he and I can track Joe down for a lesson.

Figuring it's my best shot, I call Jonathan and tell him what I've just signed up for. He says he's interested in learning too, so he reaches out to Joe and sets up a meeting.

Two days later, Jonathan and I pull up outside Joe Mystic's place in San Diego. I've never met him before, so I had no idea what to expect.

We knock, and the door opens to reveal a stocky older man with a full gray beard and mustache. We compliment him on his beard, and he grins. "Part of the act," he says, "and come Christmas, I get paid extra as a real-beard Santa. Fifty bucks an hour more than the fake-beard guys."

I've never thought about the Santa market before, but it makes sense.

As he chats, he sets up a small table. On it, he places a red fuel canister, a small metal cup, and a set of fire-eating torches—just simple threaded steel rods with oil lantern wicking wrapped around the ends.

"Alright," he says, "let's talk fire eating."

He walks us through the basics—the materials, the dangers—and how he sews the wicking onto the rods with unwaxed dental floss so a burning wick doesn't slide off and go flying. "You don't want that happening," he warns.

Then, he pours fuel into a metal cup, dips the torches, lights them, and calmly lowers the flames into his mouth. One torch goes out. Then the other.

He looks up at us. "See? It's that easy. But the key is—"

His mustache is on fire.

Just a tiny flicker at first, spreading slowly—like the fuse on a firework. And still, he talks, oblivious. I watch as the flame crawls from one clump of whiskers to the next, consuming more hair as it goes, inching toward his beard.

Jonathan and I just stood there, mesmerized. Any second now, it'll burn out on its own.

Any second...

The fire reaches his beard.

"Your beard's on fire!" we blurt out in unison.

Joe slaps his hands over his face, smothering the flames. The fire dies instantly.

"And *that* is why you don't fire eat with facial hair," he says.

We all burst out laughing. Then he finishes the lesson, wishes us luck, and even offers to send us some work if anyone asks him about jugglers.

Fifteen minutes. That's all I got.

A quick demo and a look at his setup.

On the way home, I stop at a metal supply shop and buy some ¼-inch aluminum rods, theorizing that they might dissipate heat faster than the steel ones Joe recommended. Then I hit Walmart for lantern wicking, unwaxed dental floss, sewing needles, and Coleman camp fuel.

Back home, I start assembling the torches.

The first challenge? Drilling small holes through the aluminum rods so I can thread the floss through. I snapped all my small drill bits trying.

Run to the store. Buy more bits. And snap a few more.

Eventually, I get it done.

Then I try sewing the wicking onto the rods. Turns out, this wicking stuff is *dense*. Push too hard, and the back of the needle goes straight through your finger. *So that's why people use thimbles.* I improvise with a block of wood, pressing the needle through the wick. Deep divots form in the wood from the head of the needle.

Finally, I had my first set of torches.

Time to test them.

Outside, I fill a makeshift fuel cup—just the bottom half of a cut-up soda can. I dip the smallest torch, let it soak, shake off the excess, and light it.

Alright. Commitment.

I grab the flame with my hand.

"Yeouch!"

I reflexively yank back, shaking my now-on-fire hand.

Bad move.

I'd squeezed just enough to press some fuel out of the wick, but since I didn't fully commit, I left enough oxygen for the fire to jump to my skin. Now, I'm more burned than I would've been if I'd just held on

I take a breath. Reset. *Commit this time.*

I grab the torch again, squeezing it tightly. The flame vanishes. The fire is dead. And just like that, I get it.

This is one of my first experiences with what I've come to call *stepping into it*. This, like so many things in life, requires full commitment.

Sometimes, *halfway* hurts more.

Over the next few days, I practice. I extinguish flames with my hands and manipulate them with my fingers. I even balance flaming torches on my chin.

Then, I have to face the real challenge.

The mouth extinguish.

I light a torch and bring it toward my face. The heat is *intense*. My instincts scream, *"This is a terrible idea."*

I hesitate. Then I remember Joe's words: *Heat rises.*

Tilting my head all the way back, I bring the flame down toward my mouth. Less heat. Less fear. I press it against my tongue. It tastes like a hot, sooty fireplace.

I spit repeatedly. *God, this is awful.*

But I try again. Then again. Then—

Commit.

I push the torch into my mouth and close my lips around the flame.

The fire dies instantly.

I definitely feel the burn, but far less than I expected.

Over the next week, I practice.

I push through the discomfort.

I figure out my limits.

48 hours before the actual event, I stop practicing.

Recovery is more important than a little more practice.

On the day of the show, I dress in all cotton, load my gear, and drive to the address Jim gave me.

The gig itself? Lightly attended. I perform primarily by myself. One woman watches, intrigued, and I let her touch the flame to end the set.

When I pack up and leave, no one notices.

I slip out, drive home, and go to sleep that night $200 richer. But more importantly, I had a new skill: I'd become a real-life fire-eater.

Chapter 10

Fuel to the Fire

I treated training like a full-time job, practiced hard, and even though it took a few years, all the effort eventually paid off.

My now-juggling teammate, Jonathan, and I started working under the stage name *Rootberry*. And we auditioned for, and got, a theme park gig at Legoland California. For the first time, we were real performers! And best of all, the income was stable. Now that we weren't just focused on survival, I started thinking about what could come *next*.

"How can we level up?" I wondered silently.

Instantly, the words of a fellow juggler we'd met at the juggling club began ringing in my head: *"You gotta have a gimmick."*

"Right, but what does that mean?" I wasn't sure, but I knew I had to figure it out.

We'd worked a big music festival in San Diego a few months ago, and I saw a guy swallowing swords. It was mind-blowing. I wasn't sure if it was real, but I decided right then: I'm not interested if it's just a trick. But if it's *real*... I want to learn.

Later that day, I sat down with Jonathan to discuss it. He's working on his master's degree, so it's a great time for me to take on something equally intensive.

We throw ideas back and forth.

We consider chainsaw juggling, but we can't think of a way to make it uniquely *ours*.

Sword swallowing comes up, but neither of us has any idea how to start.

Then, the idea of a body burn stunt comes up—something no one is doing.

"Any of them would be great additions to the show," Jonathan says.

Then an idea pops into my head.

"What if I juggle a chainsaw that's *on fire*, while *I'm* also on fire, and then swallow a sword *at the same time*?"

We both burst out laughing. It's ridiculous. Impossible.

Neither of us can do even *one* of those things.

We end the session no closer to an answer. But deep down, I wonder... *what if?*

After all, you gotta think big if you wanna be big.

Next morning, I start reaching out to every sword swallower I can find—not that there are many. The few responses I get are discouraging.

"It's super dangerous, don't do it."

"The liability is too great. I don't teach."

I look for books, but there are none. I search for shows featuring a sword swallower, hoping to meet one in person, but I can't find a single one.

Even the magic shops I call don't know if it's real or just a trick.

The fact that *they* don't know makes me think it might actually be real.

But nothing I try leads me any closer to answers.

So, I shift my focus to the body burn and the chainsaw.

I drive to Home Depot and buy an **Echo chainsaw with a 14-inch blade**.

It's gonna need a handle. A few phone calls later, I find a welding shop willing to build a custom-fabricated bracket and handle combo.

They built it for me, but they made it all in one piece, and I realized it was too big to pack into a travel case. So, it's back to the shop for a redesign with a removable handle.

Next, I experimented with adding cotton wicking to the blade. I found a spot on the bar—the part of the chainsaw the blade spins around—where I could drill holes without interfering with its function. I bolted some cotton wicking in place, and sure enough, when I lit it, the whole blade went up in flames.

It looks *insane*.

Now, I just have to learn to *juggle* it.

I take it to the front yard and start tossing it hand to hand.

At **18 pounds**, it's no dainty prop. I don't feel confident enough to flip it like a juggling club, so I throw it in a *flat* trajectory, hand to hand, without any spin.

For the first year, that's how I juggle the chainsaw.

Eventually, as I get more comfortable with it, I start flipping it just like I would a juggling club.

Next, I decide I need pants that can be *lit on fire*.

I dive into every resource I can find that talks about firefighters' gear. What it's made of, how it's made, anything.

I quickly learned that firefighter pants are bulky, expensive, and obviously designed for firefighting.

If I show up in a pair, people will *know* immediately that I'm wearing protective gear, which kills the effect of me spontaneously lighting on fire.

More research, until I find a company in Hollywood called Pyrotect.

They specialize in fireproof suits for race car drivers and occasionally build burn suits for movie productions.

I call and book an appointment.

In their Hollywood office, I sit across from one of their designers and explain what I want:

"I need to be able to light myself on fire, juggle a chainsaw that's also on fire, and then put myself out—all in the middle of a performance."

He tells me about fire suits, fireproof gel, and Hollywood's safety protocols, but none of it works for my situation. I won't have a team with extinguishers, I won't be covered in gel, and I need a reusable suit that can be burnt repeatedly.

He thinks for a moment, then picks up his desk phone.

"Hey, can you bring me a piece of that new fabric we just got in?"

A minute later, a woman walks in with an unremarkable-looking beige fabric.

"This doesn't offer heat protection," he explains, "but it can burn forever without deteriorating."

He pulls out a lighter and holds the flame against the fabric.

Nothing.

Even a loose thread refuses to ignite. The only trace left behind is a little soot stain.

Then he pulls out a **thin, black foam rubber-like material**. "This, on the other hand, deflects heat *really* well. But if it touches an open flame, it combusts immediately and releases thick black smoke."

He presses the two fabrics together.

"I'm thinking... if we combine these, you'll get the heat resistance from the foam and the fire resistance from the fabric. We've never done this before, but if it works, we can make a suit for you."

He holds the two layers against my hand and prepares to test them with a **propane torch** he's pulled from a desk drawer.

I hesitate. "You sure about this?"

"When it gets uncomfortable, just pull your hand back."

I consider that for a moment, then nod my assent.

The blue flame from the torch bends when it reaches the fabric.

I expect it to burn me immediately, but I feel *nothing*.

"Oh my god," I whisper. "It's amazing."

Eventually, I started to feel warmth. Then heat. Right up until—

"Okay, yeah, wow." I pull my hand back.

"That was *45 seconds*," he says. "How long do you need to burn?"

"Probably no more than 20-30 seconds."

"Then this should work."

I thought we'd cracked it right there, but it still took months of refining, re-fittings, and one close call where I couldn't get my burning legs extinguished. But in the end, we'd developed a fire act, unlike anything that'd ever come before.

I can burn for precisely **16 seconds** before it gets uncomfortable. If I push to **20 seconds**, I enter the danger zone. **23-25 seconds,** it starts to *hurt*.

30 seconds and above?

Well, you're in a *bad way*.

It was my first stunt that was genuinely new, my own invention.

I quickly learned to combine the flaming chainsaw with the body burn.

Now, when someone asks, *"Can you juggle a chainsaw?"* I'll have the perfect answer.

"Yes, I do... and I do something even crazier; I light it on fire while I'm on fire, too."

Chapter 11

Steel and Fire

I t wasn't easy figuring out how to light myself on fire and juggle a chainsaw simultaneously. It took creativity, energy, and expense to bring it to life. But once completed, it gave me what I needed to level up as a performer. I now had an act that no one else in the industry was offering. But more importantly, it gave me confidence. The confidence that comes from pushing our edge, taking a chance on failure, and ultimately succeeding. We'd laughed at the bodyburn idea in the beginning, it'd seemed impossibly far away, and now it was in the show.

How do you top that?

My desire to explore sword swallowing was as strong as ever. But without a clear path, it stayed tucked away in the back of my mind.

Then, at our second Lodi Juggling Convention, I got my breakthrough. The main show features Tony Duncan, a performer I've seen in juggling videos. His performance is exceptional, but it's how he ends his act that truly captivates me.

He swallows a sword.

I can't resist. After the show, I approached him and asked how he learned.

Tony, gracious and direct, offers a simple piece of advice: "Get a sword."

No mystical secrets, just a straightforward starting point.

As soon as the convention ends, I head west toward San Francisco.

On a previous visit to Pier 39, I'd seen a knife and sword shop, so it's my best bet for finding something to start practicing with.

When I explain my plan, the salesman raises a skeptical eyebrow but agrees to sell me a sword anyway.

As he hands me my receipt, he says, "You be careful now."

"Thanks, I will."

As I walk out of the shop, for the first time, the path to becoming a sword swallower feels like it's taking shape.

A few months later, Keith Nelson, another sword swallower, upon hearing my story of struggle, offers a few more insights.

Without these two generous individuals, I might never have learned the art of sword swallowing, and I'm forever grateful for their help.

Still, it took two years of daily practice to learn how to swallow swords. Today, I have seven world records in sword swallowing. And even with 20+ years of experience with the blade, I'm still learning to go deeper.

I didn't know it initially, but sword swallowing is so much more than a performance art—it's a practice that can be a powerful exercise in quieting the mind when approached with respect and mindfulness.

Its roots are interwoven with the practice of yoga. And today, whenever anyone asks me about learning it, my first question is, "Do you practice yoga?"

It may not seem it, but it's all the same thing, just like ice cream comes in all different flavors. Juggling, yoga, martial arts, fire handling, and sword swallowing, different as they may appear on the surface, all require the same explorations of the mind-body connection. Ever since I realized this interconnection and began speaking about it, a number of yoga studios have invited me to give lectures to their students or teachers in training. These are cherished opportunities to share the practice and my own journey within it, something I hope to do more of in the future.

I think that would be a dream—to see sword swallowing return to its one-time origins as a sacred practice, honored for the pure, beautiful meditation that it is.

I hope to teach more students to explore yoga, handle fire, and swallow swords in this beautiful way, with peace and acceptance rather than haste and force.

The students I've had, both past and present, continually prove this.

They practice, awaken, and break through.

And what they achieve in their minds is far more impressive than the physical acts of fire-manipulation and sword-swallowing themselves.

This is the reason to learn.

Not as a party trick, but rather to be what the world needs more of, awakened souls. Those who can, with a single breath, bring themselves to a place of stillness and peace.

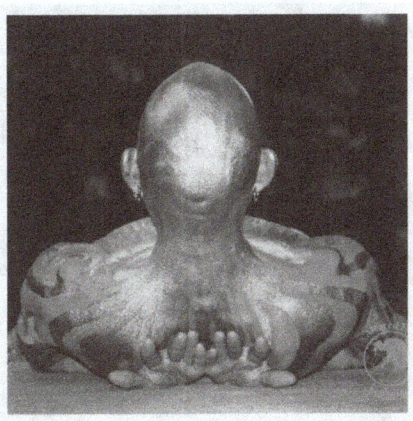

Chapter 12

Safety First

Now, where were we? Oh, yes, you said you wanted to embrace the flame? Well, let's get started!

Fire-eating is a showstopper. There's something mesmerizing about watching someone tame flames, and when it's done right, it's pure magic. But here's the thing: it's not just about the spectacle. Behind every fire-eating performance lies a deep understanding of technique and a strict commitment to safety. Every time you light something on fire, your life, the lives of your audience, the buildings and trees around you, all these things could be irreversibly changed forever. It's a <u>massive responsibility</u>, one you should never take lightly.

I'm proud to say that after doing thousands of shows, I've never hurt anyone, damaged any property, or experienced more than a few superficial burns to myself.

I want the same for you.

So let's break it down—because this isn't a party trick; it's a craft.

Personal Safety:

• **Training**: This is a non-negotiable. If you're serious about fire-eating, find a mentor. Learning from pros will save you from unnecessary injuries.

• **Protective Gear**: Fire-resistant clothing and gloves are essential. 100% cotton clothing, Kevlar, and Nomex are your friends here. Important: When polyester burns, it melts and bonds with the skin. The typical fix is to cut the skin off and use skin grafts to repair the damaged areas. <u>Fire and polyester are not friends!</u>

• **Health Precautions**: Stay sober before you perform—alcohol or drugs can impair your judgment. And hydration is key. A dehydrated body is more prone to burns.

• **Other "Flammables"**: A surprising number of everyday products can be flammable. Some lip balms, like petroleum jelly, hair products, like hair spray, and probably 1000 more items, making up a list too verbose to attempt to catalog here, may readily catch on fire. You'll have to use your common sense and cultivate the ability to foresee potential hazards to do this safely. See your scenario with new eyes, fire eyes, and imagine what could go wrong. Then make corrections and omissions until all these imagined scenarios are mitigated.

Equipment Safety:

• **Quality Materials**: Always use professional-grade fire equipment. Low-quality wands can fail at the worst time, and that's a safety hazard.

• **Proper Fuel**: Use only safe fuels like paraffin or white gas. These burn clean and at manageable temperatures, unlike other flammable liquids.

Performance Safety:

• **Venue Prep**: Clear the area of flammable materials and ensure there's enough ventilation. Have fire extinguishers. Have fire blankets on hand, buckets of water, or a trigger-actuated nozzle-capped garden hose turned on and ready for deployment. You're performing with fire, so these precautions are a must.

• **Audience Safety**: Keep your audience at a safe distance (requirements vary by state or region). No matter how amazing your skills are, safety should always come first.

Emergency Readiness:

• **First Aid**: You should know the basics of first aid and have a kit nearby. Better safe than sorry.

• **Emergency Plan**: Always have an emergency plan, know the nearest exits, and make sure your team knows their roles in an emergency.

Professionalism:

• **Insurance and Local Regulations**: Different cities, states, and countries have differing rules in place regarding fire manipulation. You must do your own due diligence to ensure you are complying with local laws. The same goes for insurance. Strive to uphold the utmost professionalism in every aspect of your exploration.

Above all, never push beyond what you're comfortable with or what you can perform confidently:

There may come a day when you're hired to perform, the client is excited, the audience is waiting, and you notice a serious safety concern. In that moment, you must speak up, ensure it's addressed, and, if necessary, refuse to perform. This isn't about ego—it's about protecting lives. If you allow yourself to be pressured into an unsafe situation and something goes wrong, it will be your name and face in the headlines. Stand your ground. You must be as courageous in these moments as you are each time you embrace the flame.

Chapter 13

Tools of the Flame

Equipment for Fire Eating and Fire Manipulation:

A round the world, fire manipulation takes on many forms, each shaped by culture, resources, and performer preference. From ancient ceremonial displays to modern-day stage and street performances, artists have developed various tools and techniques. There is no single "right way" to work with fire. What you'll read here are not rigid rules, but field-tested recommendations — methods I have successfully used. These guidelines aim to help you build a solid, safe foundation for your own journey into the fire arts.

The Essentials:

Fuel

The most common fuels for fire eating and manipulation are **Coleman Camp Fuel (naphtha)** and **lamp oil (paraffin-based)**. Each has its pros and cons, and you should understand the differences:

• Coleman Camp Fuel

Burns bright and clean, making it ideal for performance, but it is also highly volatile. It ignites easily and evaporates quickly, which can be both a blessing and a hazard.

• Lamp Oil

Burns at a lower temperature and is generally more forgiving, especially for beginners, though it tends to smoke more and may leave an oily residue.

Never use fuels like gasoline, lighter fluid, or alcohol-based products. They are dangerous and unpredictable in this context.

Torch Construction

A good fire-eating torch typically consists of a **non-flammable handle** (often aluminum, steel, or another heat-resistant metal) and a **wicking material** at the tip. The wicking is usually made of Kevlar, cotton lantern wicking/cord (I've even seen someone use cotton balls wrapped in unwaxed dental floss, but I wouldn't recommend it), and each has its own burn profile. Kevlar lasts longer, but cotton is easier to light and extinguish, often making it better for beginners.

Note: A full instructional video on making your own fire-eating torches is coming soon and will be available exclusively to my higher-tier Patreon members.

Fuel Container

You'll need a sealable **metal container** for holding your fuel. This container will double as a **dipping station** for soaking your torches between burns.

Metal military-style ammo cans are a popular choice: They're durable, seal tightly, and are easy to transport. Triple-check that it doesn't leak through; the seals are not always foolproof.

Set up your fueling station **far away from your performance or practice area**. Yes, walking back and forth to dip your torches might be inconvenient, but it's far less inconvenient than going to the hospital or explaining to firefighters why your garage is now missing a wall.

Fire Source

Bring at least **one reliable lighter**. Many professionals carry backups—windproof lighters, grill lighters, or even torches with a built-in ignition system. Whatever you use, make sure you're confident in it and that it works in your environment (outdoors, windy, humid, etc.).

Safety Equipment

When working with fire, **redundancy in safety is not paranoia — it's professionalism.** You should always have:

• A **fire extinguisher** (CO_2 preferred)

• A **fire blanket**

• A **water source** like a **garden hose with a nozzle** that allows it to be activated without a constant flow

CO_2 extinguishers are ideal because they don't leave behind powder residue or cause skin irritation, which some standard household extinguishers can. But multipurpose (ABC) extinguishers are most common.

Keep all of your safety equipment **visible, accessible, and tested**. This isn't just for your own safety — if something goes wrong and someone else needs to help you, they shouldn't have to dig through a toolbox to find what could save your life.

As your fire proficiency grows, you will see people disregarding some, or all, of these safety precautions. These people might be fellow flow artists or even professional practitioners. They might even tell you that you're worrying too much, that you need to loosen up. If this happens, don't give in to the pressure. They can take those chances if they wish, but you must conduct yourself professionally and safely every time.

Chapter 14

Fire Manipulation Torches!

If you need torches and don't want to tackle making them yourself. Handmade fire-manipulation torches are available through my Etsy store, **itemsthatintrigue**. Whether you're just starting your journey into fire performance or looking to upgrade your gear, these torches are crafted for reliability and performance.

Pricing:
• Set of two torches – $70*

(*Current prices may differ as availability, material costs, or other variables change.)

While on the Etsy store, check out the other unique items that intrigue you, including vintage typewriters and, soon, specially made **sword-swallowing swords** for serious practitioners.

If fire calls you, maybe this is your sign to answer it. 🔥

Tap into the mystery.

Master the art.

Equip yourself with the right tools.

itemsthatintrigue on etsy:

Embracing the Flame

Chapter 15

Beyond Instinct

It was a warm, still afternoon at the St. Pete Micro Farm. The mulberry tree above us had been dropping fruit all week, staining the concrete table in deep purples and reds. That table had seen a lot—meals, meetings, moments of insight—but today, it witnessed something a little more primal.

I was working with Dr. Cath, a new student I'd begun mentoring in the basics of fire manipulation and fire eating. We stood together in the backyard, surrounded by fruit trees and the soft clucking of free-range chickens. The air smelled faintly of mulch, blossoms, and just a little bit like... petroleum naphtha.

I held up a lit torch. "Let's talk about your nervous system," I said, "and why it's not always telling you the truth."

She raised an eyebrow, curious but understandably cautious.

"You see," I continued, "our nerves and pain receptors are *reflexive*. They're instantaneous. They're hardwired for survival. If you touch something like a red-hot piece of metal—say, the end of a drill bit that's been spinning at high speed—your nerves send a message to your brain that screams *danger!* And they're right. That kind of heat can brand you instantly. There's no room for hesitation."

"But," I said, holding the torch closer, "fire's not always like that. The kind of fuel we use here burns at a much lower temperature than glowing metal. You actually have a small window of time where, yes, it might *hurt*, but it won't cause real damage—*if* you know what you're doing."

She leaned in, but hesitated. Instinct pulling her back.

I nodded. "This is where the yogic principle of *pratyahara* comes in—*the denial of the senses.* It's the conscious decision to override what your body is screaming at you. Because in this case, your body doesn't have the full story. You do."

"Touch the flame," I said gently.

Her hand moved, hovered, then made contact with the edge of the flame. She immediately recoiled. "Ouch!"

But before I could respond, she laughed. "Wait—that wasn't bad. No, really, that wasn't bad at all!"

There it is, I thought. The shift. The *breakthrough moment*—where understanding overcomes reflex, and a human being steps into power they didn't know they had.

By the end of that first session, Dr. Cath was extinguishing flames with her bare hands. She passed fire up and down her arms. She transferred it from one torch to another using just her fingers. She even performed a mouth extinguish—putting literal fire into her face, trusting herself and her training to know what her instincts didn't.

And it was then, as we sat back down at the purple-streaked table, still breathing in the scent of flame and fuel, that she said it:

"Our instincts are not always the complete story."

That one sentence hit me like a gong. Because she was absolutely right.

Our bodies are designed to protect us. Pain receptors exist to keep us alive. And thank goodness they do! But they're not intelligent. They can't distinguish between something that will hurt us *instantly* and something that will only hurt us *eventually*. They just yell *danger* without nuance.

That's the difference between putting your hand on a red-hot pan and putting out a flame. The former destroys tissue in milliseconds. The latter—if done correctly—*feels* dangerous but *isn't*.

And it's not just fire. This applies across our entire lives.

Are you scared to ask your boss for a raise? That's fear, not fact.

Do you panic behind the wheel when traffic gets heavy? That's your nervous system going into autopilot.

Do you avoid ocean swims because you're afraid of sharks? Same wiring—overactive instincts, under-informed by reality.

Your brain is a computer. It runs patterns. It acts on impulse. And if you let it take the wheel completely—if you live entirely in reflex mode—you'll miss out on the magic of deliberate living.

The solution isn't to *ignore* your instincts. It's to *question* them. Interrogate them. Test whether the fear is justified or simply outdated.

Even in smaller things, like impulse shopping, one of my students used to struggle with buying things she didn't need. So we made a rule: if it wasn't on her list when she walked into the store, she wasn't allowed to buy it. But she *could* write it down. If she was still thinking about it a week later, she could return and get it.

That's pratyahara in action. Denial of the senses, not as punishment, but as power.

Of course, not everything in life needs to be micromanaged. I make my morning coffee the exact same way every day—five ice cubes, oat milk, Hershey's syrup. It's a routine that doesn't need disruption because it doesn't get in the way of what I want in life.

But the question we all have to ask ourselves is:

Where is your reflex running the show—and where is it holding you back from your higher potential?

Fire teaches us this with brutal clarity. You *will* feel pain. But not every pain means you're being harmed. Sometimes, pain is just the body's primitive alarm system ringing inappropriately.

And when we can stand calmly in the fire—when we can override that instinct with intention—that's where transformation begins.

Chapter 16

❧ *Techniques* ❧

Fire manipulation might look effortless when it's done right, but it takes tons of practice to get to that point. There are a few core techniques that every fire handler needs to master.

1. Handling Fire:

• **Fire Wands**: These are essential. You've got your metal or wood wand with a wick soaked in flammable liquid—think cotton or Kevlar. The key here is managing the temperature and flame, which is crucial for safety and performance. (Torches available through our Etsy shop, **itemsthatintrigue**)

• **Twirling & Spinning**: When you get good at it, twirling and spinning fire wands becomes a dynamic part of the act, adding layers of movement and excitement that draw in the audience.

2. Extinguishing Flames:

• **Hand Extinguish:** This technique involves wrapping the flame in your hand, effectively denying it oxygen to snuff it out. By creating a seal around the wick with your fingers, you can safely extinguish the flame without using your lips or mouth. It requires a high level of control and timing, as you must close off the airflow at just the right moment to ensure the fire goes out without causing harm. Precision here is key to mastering the skill.

🔥 **A common mistake new performers make is overburning their torches — allowing the fuel to completely burn off before extinguishing the flame. When this happens, the wick itself begins to smolder. If a smoldering torch is dipped back into the fuel, it can ignite the entire container, creating a catastrophic fire hazard. Always extinguish your torches before they run dry.** 🔥

Tips:

- **Always shake excess fuel out of dipped torches.**
- **Practice 50 "extinguishes" with an unlit torch, ensuring all wicking is covered.**
- **Once lit, lightly tap the torch against your hand, and get comfortable.**
- **When ready, commitment is key; it takes a moment to fully extinguish the flame.**
- **Limit practice, after a few extinguishes, the protective oils on your hand will be burned away.**
- **Extra Credit - Try extinguishing with both hands.**

Hover Torch

Place in Hand

• **Mouth Extinguish:** In this advanced technique, you carefully place the wick into your mouth, using the lack of oxygen to extinguish the flame. It's a showy method that demands confidence and practice. If you're not trained, this can be risky, so it's not something to attempt casually.

Tips:

- **Make sure your head is tilted very far back while attempting.**
- **Practice on windless days, or with the wind to your back.**
- **At first, lightly tap the torch against your tongue, baby steps.**
- **Refresh the saliva coating on your tongue after each touch with the torch.**
- **Try gently exhaling to control the heat and intensity of the flame.**
- **When ready, place the torch on the outstretched tongue and pull the tongue in as a guide.**
- **NEVER inhale while fire is in, around, or near your face.**

• **Fire Transfers:** Once you're comfortable with extinguishing the flame, you can take it a step further by transferring the fire from one wand to another or even to your mouth. This creates the illusion of "eating" the fire, and it's a visual thrill for the audience. It's one of the most exciting and dynamic elements of the performance!

Tips:

- **Best attempted when the torch is freshly fueled and still "cool."**
- **Squeeze the lit torch to acquire a small amount of fuel on the fingertips.**
- **Move lit fingers steadily to retain the delicate flame.**
- **Hold torch tips close to each other so the transfer distance is minimal.**

Advanced Techniques for Veteran Fire Manipulators:

• **Fire Blasts (Extremely Dangerous**): For this stunt, the practitioner takes **lamp oil** into the mouth (never use Coleman Camp Fuel), they then expel a fine mist toward a held flame to create a fireball. It's a balance of precision and timing—get it wrong or fail to employ strong safety practices, and it can go bad quickly. YouTube has hundreds of videos depicting people who have lit themselves on fire after they grew overconfident in their ability to blow fire. I encourage you to search out some of these videos and embrace the lessons they have to teach. More than any other, this stunt is responsible for fire-eating injuries and accidents. **Warning: You must seek out an instructor to learn this. Just having fuel in the mouth is hazardous. Accidentally swallowing fuel is hazardous. Improper blast technique can cause you to light on fire. Aerating fuel can be deadly (inhalation of fuel into the lungs).**

  • **Body Burns**: Some performers take it to the next level and incorporate controlled burns on parts of their bodies (arms, hands, legs, whole body). It's an amazing display but comes with huge risks, so it's not for the faint of heart.

This is just a short list—the number of tricks a fire manipulator can explore is vast. One could train for years and still not master them all. I encourage you to grow slowly, remain humble, seek guidance, and always exercise all possible safety protocols. I want you to live to be a wise old fire-handler.

Chapter 17

Smoldering Embers

Thank you

This manual, along with training, is a solid foundation —but it's just the beginning. Mastery comes through patience. Fire rewards those who respect the process and commit to growth without rushing the journey.

Safety must always be your priority. Stay aware, use the right equipment, and never ignore the fundamentals. Fire is beautiful, exhilarating, and unforgiving. If in doubt, don't light up. Always err on the side of caution.

I want to see you keep growing. Learning the moves is one thing; embodying the art is another. You don't have to do it alone. I've spent decades refining these techniques, and I'm here to help guide your journey.

To go deeper, join me on Patreon (@mrbillberry). There, you'll find exclusive lessons, behind-the-scenes insights, and a community of artists pushing boundaries safely and creatively. It's where we can grow together.

Before you go, I want to leave you with this:

Manipulating fire isn't as hard as it seems. What makes it difficult is our perception—our fear, our assumptions, our story about what fire is. I hope that through this book and your practice, you begin to rewrite that story. To form a new relationship with fire, one rooted in presence, control, and deep respect.

Once you've learned to tame the flame outside of you, something powerful begins to happen: you start to face the fire within. The same discipline, awareness, and courage you've built through fire handling can serve you in mastering the internal flame—the one that fuels your drive, your creativity, and your purpose.

That's what *Embracing the Flame* is really about. Not just learning a daring skill, but transforming through it, becoming someone who meets intensity with calm, chaos with clarity, and fear with presence.

Now take a deep breath and trust yourself. The fire's waiting.

—Mr. Bill Berry

To support your journey beyond the written word, the first 999 purchasers of this book receive a **free 3-month subscription** ($150 value) to the Mr. Bill Berry Patreon. This is not a sales pitch — it's a continuation of your training. Patreon is where you'll find video demonstrations, expanded techniques, and deeper explorations of the practices described in this manual.

I encourage you to take advantage of these resources and watch the techniques in action. This content is designed to help you go further, safer, and more confidently as you embrace the flame.

Redeem your **3 months** of access to the Mr. Bill Berry Patreon community today!

https://www.patreon.com/Mr.BillBerry/redeem/9E03C

Embracing the Flame

Chapter 18

One-on-One Fire Training

Ready to take your practice to the next level?

I now offer **personalized, one-on-one fire training sessions**—available **in person** or **virtually**—through my Patreon page at Mr.billberry. These exclusive sessions are designed for serious students ready to commit to excellence, safety, and growth.

Each session includes:
- ✓ **A one-hour intensive** tailored to your experience level
- ✓ **Step-by-step coaching** as I walk you through technique, mindset, and personal breakthroughs
- ✓ **Custom evaluation** of your practice, performance space, fuel selection, and safety protocols

This is more than just a lesson—it's a mentorship in mastering the art responsibly. Whether you're starting out or looking to refine your approach, I'll help you **conquer your fears, sharpen your technique, and fortify your safety setup**.

Important Note:

Due to the nature of this art, **safety is non-negotiable**. All sessions—virtual or in-person—require that you have:

- 🔥 A well-ventilated **outdoor** practice space
- 🔥 Appropriate **fuel, fuel container, and tools**
- 🔥 **Fire safety gear and protocols** in place (including a fire blanket and extinguisher)

All students must be 18 years of age or older and show identification for verification.

If I see *anything* unsafe in your setup, I will **pause or cancel the session** until the proper conditions are met. This is for your protection—and the protection of anyone nearby.

Your transformation begins when you commit. Check out Patreon.com/Mr.billberry for **current pricing and availability**, and let's light the path forward—**safely, skillfully, and spectacularly**.

Also by Bill Berry

Stories That Move, **238 pages.**

Available on Amazon: https://a.co/d/onAudJe

Compact, earnest, and absorbing." - Kirkus Reviews

"Humane, harrowing stories of a life facing violence and danger." - Booklife.com

"The stories absolutely move." - Publishers Weekly

The BookLife Prize Review:

Plot/Idea: Berry shares snippets of his childhood through adulthood, recollections that, at times, are intensely honest and vulnerable. He embeds a life lesson in each of his dispensed memories—a collection that will speak to readers who appreciate simple, but crucial, aha moments.

Prose: Berry writes with a cinematic flair, crafting scenes that are stunningly vivid and lifelike. His down-to-earth style pairs well with his straightforward wisdom.

Originality: The distinction of Berry's memoir lies in his skillful storytelling;

his adventures are rendered clearly, with an animated spirit that infuses the book with incredible energy.

Character/Execution: This memoir is well-structured and easy to digest. Berry's reminiscences resonate, offering insight alongside vibrant tokens of his intriguing past experiences.

About:

If you've ever been bullied and wondered how to better handle those situations, this is for you.

If you wrestle with difficult family dynamics, this book is for you.

If you're ready to laugh out loud, this book is for you.

Stories That Move is a collection of compelling, raw tales documenting the author's journey. From the first page to the last, you'll be drawn into the human experience at a depth few authors can traverse. And in so doing, you'll discover things about yourself.

This book is like a power-up; it's filled with experiences, truth, and emotion. And like life, we can't predict what will be on the next page. As you read, you'll be pushed, you'll feel empowered, you'll see your own journey in a new light. And after you've reached the end, you'll find that you've grown in understanding, love, trust, and forgiveness. The humanity revealed in each of these stories will give you a deeper view into yourself.

What People Are Saying:

"These stories belong beside the most prolific writers of our time. This is worthy of the New Yorker" ∼ Jim S.

"Reading his work draws me into something unexpected and profound." ∼ Susan L.

"Well, he made me cry, so that's mission accomplished" ∼ Penn J.

"A truly unique book filled with tons of short stories with meaningful messages. I could not stop reading it! It is truly a wonderful book filled with short, relatable stories that are about everything we experience in life...and more than some experience! The author is raw and does not hold back from telling some of his most personal experiences that you are sure to relate to in one way or another. You won't want to stop reading it! Get it now! You are going to love it!" ∼ Rick

If you enjoy memoirs, short stories, first-person accounts, psychology, or philosophy, or want a thought-provoking title for your next book club, *Stories That Move* is a great choice.

Coming Soon: *The Creative's Guide to Conquering the Self -*
Winter 2025

A bold manifesto for artists, performers, dreamers, and doers ready to stop waiting for permission and start building the life they imagine. Blending real-world experience with raw, actionable insight, this book delivers battle-tested strategies for making your passion sustainable—without selling your soul. Whether you're a juggler, filmmaker, writer, fire handler, or idea alchemist of any kind, this guide is your invitation to rise up, make art that matters, and take your rightful place in the arena.

Coming Soon: Embark on an extraordinary journey with *Sick Kid* - Summer 2026

A captivating memoir by Mr. Bill Berry. Delve into a childhood shaped by a challenging heart condition and an unexpected path to healing under the tutelage of Dr. Raja Singham, a Sri Lankan cardiologist and master of Eastern Philosophy. Witness how ancient wisdom not only offered control over a faltering heartbeat but also laid the foundation for a life of profound purpose. From discipline honed through sword swallowing to a transformative awakening experience on the yoga mat, "Sick Kid" unveils the unlikely convergence of seemingly disparate philosophies. This is the story of forging an exceptional path, embracing the unconventional, and discovering unity in the most unexpected of places.

About the Author

Bill Berry lives in Saint Petersburg, Florida, with his wife, two curious cats, and a spirited flock of ten chickens. When he's not performing jaw-dropping feats onstage, he's nurturing a quieter kind of magic in his backyard. As the co-founder of the St. Pete Micro Farm, an urban agricultural project built on just one-tenth of an acre, Bill has transformed his home into a thriving example of sustainable, edible landscaping—featuring over 80 species of fruiting trees and shrubs.

Equal parts artist, adventurer, and cultivator of growth—both in the soil and in people—Bill is passionate about building community, living deliberately, and turning life's challenges into creative fuel. *Embracing the Flame* is yet another expression of that ethos: a continuation of a life devoted to exploration, transformation, and helping others uncover their own fire within.

Find me online to continue the journey. Search mrbillberry on most socials, or visit www.mrbillberry.com

www.ingramcontent.com/pod-product-compliance
Lightning Source LLC
Chambersburg PA
CBHW071522120626
46550CB00006B/2321